In the Spotlight™

Volume 1

Levels D–F

Henry Billings
Melissa Billings

 Glencoe

New York, New York   Columbus, Ohio   Chicago, Illinois   Peoria, Illinois   Woodland Hills, California

JAMESTOWN EDUCATION

Glencoe

The *McGraw-Hill* Companies

ISBN-13: 978-0-07-874319-1
ISBN-10: 0-07-874319-2

Send all queries to:
Glencoe/McGraw-Hill
8787 Orion Place
Columbus, OH 43240-4027

2 3 4 5 6 7 8 9 10 021 10 09 08 07

Contents

Unit Three

To the Student

This book has nine articles about celebrities, or famous people, in the world today. Some of the celebrities are movie or television stars. Some are sports players. Others are authors or musicians.

The lives of these stars can inspire us. Some of the stars had tough times while growing up. They worked very hard to find success. Others had to stay focused on their dreams even when other people thought they would fail. And some had to get through challenges even after they became well-known.

In this book you will work on these three specific reading skills:

Main Idea and Supporting Details

Sequence

Author's Viewpoint

You will also work on other reading and vocabulary skills. This will help you understand and think about what you read. The lessons include types of questions often found on state and national tests. Completing the questions can help you get ready for tests you may have to take later.

How to Use This Book

About the Book

This book has three units. Each unit has three lessons. Each lesson has an article about a celebrity followed by practice exercises.

Working Through Each Lesson

Photo Start each lesson by looking at the photo. Read the title and subtitle to get an idea of what the article will focus on.

Think About What You Know, Word Power, Reading Skill This page will help you prepare to read.

Article Now read about the celebrity. Enjoy!

Activities Complete all the activities. Then check your work. Your teacher will give you an answer key to do this. Record the number of your correct answers for each activity. At the end of the lesson, add up your total score for parts A, B, and C. Then find your percentage score in the table. Record your percentage score on the Comprehension and Critical Thinking Progress Graph on page 105.

Compare and Contrast Chart At the end of each unit you will complete a Compare and Contrast Chart. The chart will help you see what some of the celebrities in the unit have in common.

My Personal Dictionary In the back of this book, you can jot down words you would like to know more about. Later you can ask your teacher or a classmate what the words mean. Then you can add the definitions in your own words.

Jamie Foxx

Derek Jeter

Lucy Liu

Jamie Foxx
A Man with Many Talents

Birth Name Eric Morlon Bishop
Birth Date and Place December 13, 1967, Terrell, Texas
Home Los Angeles, California

Think About What You Know

Have you ever worked toward one thing but then decided to do something else? Read the article to find out why Jamie Foxx changed his career plans.

Word Power

What do the words below tell you about the article?

achieve to complete something successfully

impersonations acts of copying other people's voices and movements

comedy the art of making people laugh

nominated suggested for an award

beloved much loved

Reading Skill

Main Idea and Supporting Details The most important idea in a paragraph is the **main idea.** Each sentence in the paragraph will be about the main idea. These sentences are called **supporting details.** In some paragraphs, the writer states the main idea in one sentence.

Example	
Main Idea	Musicians and actors have a lot in common.
Supporting Details	Both musicians and actors perform in front of live audiences or cameras. Acting well and playing music well both require talent and practice.

"Musicians and actors have a lot in common" is the main idea. Can you give two reasons why this is the main idea?

Jamie Foxx

A Man with Many Talents

Jamie Foxx's mother was just a teenager when he was born. She had little money, few skills, and an unstable marriage. As Foxx puts it, "She wasn't ready for responsibility." By the time Foxx was seven months old, his mother was ready to give him up. But at that moment his grandmother, Estelle Talley, stepped in.

2   "My grandmother was 60 years old when she adopted me," Foxx says. Her age didn't matter, however. What mattered was that she saw something special in the child. "She saw me reading early, saw I was smart, and believed I was born to **achieve** truly special things."

3   Talley made sure Foxx read lots of books, went to church, and learned to play the piano. She made him join the Boy Scouts and sing with the church choir. To teach him about the world outside their small town of Terrell, Texas, she took him on bus trips to Canada and Florida.

4   Under her guidance, Foxx blossomed. He got good grades in school and became a star football player on the high school team. He not only directed the church choir but also led a local band called Leather and Lace. He mastered the drums and the trumpet. In addition, he became very good on the piano.

5   Believe it or not, that wasn't all. On top of everything else, Foxx was very funny. Even as a young boy, he had the ability to make people laugh. He was so good at it that, in second grade, his teacher would sometimes reward the students by letting Foxx stand up and tell them jokes.

6   Foxx graduated from high school in 1986. He won a scholarship to study classical piano at a college in San Diego. He spent two years there, playing with some of the most talented young musicians in the world. Then, in 1988, he left, hoping to break into the music business.

7   Soon after leaving school, Foxx went to a **comedy** club with a friend. Because it was an "open mike" night, anyone could stand up and perform. Foxx's friend dared him to give it a try. Foxx went onstage and began doing **impersonations** of famous people. He did Ronald Reagan, Bill Cosby, and several others. The audience loved him. And he loved being in the spotlight. At that moment, he decided to switch careers. He decided to become a stand-up comic.

8   Over the next couple of years, Foxx polished his act. He worked in a shoe store to pay the bills, but he performed at comedy clubs whenever he could. He often went to Amateur Nights, where club managers would pick performers from a list of names.

9   At that time, Foxx was still using his birth name, Eric Bishop. But he noticed that most of the comics at Amateur Nights were men. "Three girls would show up and 22 guys would show up," says Foxx. Because the managers wanted a mix of performers, the women would all get to perform. So Foxx thought up some names that could be either male or female. These included Tracey Green, Stacy King, and Jamie Foxx.

Skill Break
Main Idea and Supporting Details

Look at paragraph 5 on page 4. The paragraph gives **details** about Foxx's talents. Even as a boy, Foxx had the ability to make people laugh. His second-grade teacher would reward the students by letting Foxx tell them jokes. These **details** support the **main idea.**

What is the **main idea** of the paragraph?

10   One Amateur Night he wrote these names down on the list. He hoped the club manager would pick one, thinking it was a woman's name. And that's exactly what happened. "They picked Jamie Foxx," he recalls. He went onstage under that name and dazzled the crowd. So he gave up being Eric Bishop and stayed with Jamie Foxx. "I loved my old name," he says. "But Eric Bishop was Clark Kent. And Jamie Foxx is Superman."

11   In 1991 Foxx won a part on the TV show *In Living Color*. There Foxx created a very funny character named Wanda. Audiences loved it. And they loved him in *The Jamie Foxx Show,* which ran from 1996 to 2001.

12   Foxx knew he was a great comic. But he still loved music. So in 1994 he put out his first album, *Peep This*. Every song on it was written, sung, and produced by Foxx himself.

13   Fox also believed he could be a serious actor. So he began going after parts in serious movies. His first really good role came in 1999. He played a football player in *Any Given Sunday.* After that, Foxx got good roles in several other films.

14   Then, in 2004, Foxx had an amazing year. That year he appeared in not one but four films. The first was the TV movie *Redemption,* in which he plays a former gang member. The second was *Breakin' All the Rules,* which he stars in. The third was *Collateral,* starring Tom Cruise. There Foxx plays a taxi driver who is forced to drive a hit man around town. And the biggest was *Ray,* a movie about Ray Charles.

▶ Foxx spells his name with two *x*'s to honor the late African American actor Redd Foxx.

▶ He began taking piano lessons when he was three years old.

▶ He was a star football player in high school.

Jamie Foxx poses with his 2005 Academy Award for Best Actor.

15   Foxx won praise for his work in all four films. In fact, he became the first person ever to be **nominated** for three Golden Globe Awards in one year. But it was his role as Ray Charles that earned him the most fame. Everyone agreed that Foxx was terrific in this movie. To prepare for the role, he lost 25 pounds. He had his eyes glued shut for many hours during the day. He did this so he could understand what it was like to be blind, as Charles was. And he practiced the piano until he could play the way Charles did.

16   Foxx's role as Ray Charles earned him the 2005 Academy Award for Best Actor. He had certainly come a long way from his tough beginning back in Terrell, Texas. Walking up onto the stage to collect his award, Foxx was well aware of this. He remembered his **beloved** grandmother, Estelle Talley, who had died a few months earlier. "She was my first acting teacher," he told the crowd. "She said, 'Act like you've got some sense . . . Act like you've been someplace.'" Then, fighting back tears, Foxx said, "She still talks to me now, only now she talks to me in my dreams. And I can't wait to go to sleep tonight because we have a lot to talk about."

A Understanding What You Read

◆ Fill in the circle next to each correct answer.

1. Why did Foxx's grandmother take him on bus trips?

○ A. to visit comedy clubs in Canada and Florida

○ B. to learn about the world outside Terrell, Texas

○ C. to study classical piano at a college in San Diego

2. What caused Eric Bishop to first use the name Jamie Foxx?

○ A. He wanted people to think of him as a serious actor.

○ B. He wanted a manager to think it was a woman's name.

○ C. He wanted to have a good name for the music business.

3. How did Foxx prepare for his role in the movie *Ray?*

○ A. He recorded *Peep This.*

○ B. He learned to drive a taxi.

○ C. He lost 25 pounds.

4. From what you read in paragraph 16, which of these is probably true?

○ A. Foxx misses his grandmother very much.

○ B. Foxx would like to move back to Texas.

○ C. Foxx often has trouble sleeping.

5. What lesson about life does this article teach?

○ A. If you fail in one career, you can always try another one.

○ B. Laughter is one of the greatest gifts we can give to others.

○ C. A loving caregiver can make a big difference for a child.

_____ Number of Correct Answers: Part A

B   Finding the Main Idea and Supporting Details

◆ **Read each paragraph below. Fill in the circle next to the sentence that best states the main idea for each paragraph.**

1.

   Then, in 2004, Foxx had an amazing year. That year he appeared in not one but four films. The first was the TV movie *Redemption,* in which he plays a former gang member. The second was *Breakin' All the Rules,* which he stars in. The third was *Collateral,* starring Tom Cruise. There Foxx plays a taxi driver who is forced to drive a hit man around town. And the biggest was *Ray,* a movie about Ray Charles.

   ○ A. The biggest was a movie about Ray Charles.
   ○ B. Foxx appeared in four great films.
   ○ C. In 2004 Foxx had an amazing year.

2.

   Foxx won praise for his work in all four films. In fact, he became the first person ever to be nominated for three Golden Globe Awards in one year. But it was his role as Ray Charles that earned him the most fame. Everyone agreed that Foxx was terrific in this movie. To prepare for the role, he lost 25 pounds. He had his eyes glued shut for many hours during the day. He did this so he could understand what it was like to be blind, as Charles was. And he practiced the piano until he could play the way Charles did.

   ○ A. To prepare for the role, he lost 25 pounds.
   ○ B. Foxx won praise for his work in all four films.
   ○ C. Everyone agreed that Foxx was terrific in *Ray*.

_____ Number of Correct Answers: Part B

C Using Words

◆ **Complete each sentence with a word from the box. Write the missing word on the line.**

achieve	comedy	beloved
impersonations	nominated	

1. My painting was _____ for an art award.

2. He looked and sounded just like the other kids when he did

_____ of them.

3. I watch _____ shows when I want to laugh.

4. Their _____ dog had been part of the family
for years.

5. You never know what you can _____ until you try.

◆ **Choose one word from the box. Write a new sentence using the word.**

6. word: _____

_____

_____

_____ Number of Correct Answers: Part C

D Writing About It

Write a Speech

◆ Write a speech about Jamie Foxx that describes his work in the movie *Ray*. Finish the sentences below to write your speech. Use the checklist on page 103 to check your work.

I would like to tell you about Jamie Foxx and his great movie

Ray. Foxx used his musical training in this movie when he _____

_____ .

To look more like Ray Charles, Foxx had to _____

_____ .

But it was worth it. His performance in *Ray* earned him _____

_____ .

Lesson 1 Add your correct answers from parts A, B, and C to get your total score. Then find the percentage for your total score on the chart below. Record your percentage on the graph on page 105.

_____ Total Score for Parts A, B, and C

_____ Percentage

Total Score	1	2	3	4	5	6	7	8	9	10	11	12	13
Percentage	8	15	23	31	38	46	54	62	69	77	85	92	100

Derek Jeter
Baseball's Number-One Good Guy

Birth Name Derek Sanderson Jeter

Birth Date and Place June 26, 1974, Pequannock, New Jersey

Homes New York City and Tampa, Florida

Think About What You Know

Have you ever wanted to help people in need? Whom would you help? How would you help them? Read the article to find out what Derek Jeter does to help young people.

Word Power

What do the words below tell you about the article?

drafted chosen to play on a professional team

rookie a first-year player in a professional sport

contract an agreed-upon plan

charity a group that helps people in need

potential a natural ability that might grow into something more

Reading Skill

Sequence The order of events in a story or an article is called **sequence.** The author will not always use signal words such as *first* and *then*. Sometimes you must use what you know and clues from the text to find the sequence.

Example	
The First Event	She joined the team when she was a junior.
The Next Event	During her senior year, she became the team captain.

"She joined the team" is the first event in the sequence. The second event is "she became the team captain." How might you use the clues in the text and what you already know to find this sequence?

Derek Jeter
Baseball's Number-One Good Guy

What is it about Derek Jeter? Why does everybody like this New York Yankees shortstop? Even people in Boston can't find anything bad to say about him, and Boston baseball fans are raised from birth to dislike the Yankees! There are two reasons why Jeter is so popular. First there's what he does on the field. He always gives his best effort, and he always acts responsibly. Then there's what he does off the field. He is one of the kindest people you could ever hope to meet.

2   Jeter fell in love with baseball while growing up in Michigan. He played it every chance he got. By high school, he was a star player. After graduating in 1992, he had a choice. He could play baseball in college, or he could turn professional right away. He was **drafted** by his favorite team, the Yankees, so he decided to give up his spot in college and go straight into baseball.

3   Jeter started in the low minor leagues. Still a teenager, he found it hard to adjust to life as a minor leaguer. He missed home, and that hurt his game. In his first season, he hit just .202. He improved the next year, hitting .293. After that Jeter continued to get better and better. He got so good, in fact, that *Sporting News* named him Minor League Player of the Year in 1994.

4   In 1995 he divided his time between the minor leagues and the Yankees. At last, in 1996, he joined the Yankees full-time. Joe Torre, the manager, told him the shortstop job was his. Jeter didn't let Torre down. He hit .314 and played very well in the field. As a result, Jeter was named American League **Rookie** of the Year. In addition, his team won the World Series that year. Led by Jeter, the Yankees would win the World Series three more times over the next four years.

5   Jeter doesn't have the big home run numbers of some other stars. His game is not based on power. It is not based on any one skill. He does everything well. His all-around play has won him the respect of his teammates. "He's the best player I've ever played with," says former Yankees outfielder Paul O'Neill. "What sets him apart is the number of ways he can affect a game."

6   In other words, Jeter can find lots of ways to defeat his opponents. He is especially tough when the score is very close. He can make the one play that turns a game around. It may be a diving catch into the stands. It may be a key stolen base. Or it may be a clutch hit in the bottom of the ninth inning. Sometimes it is something as simple as a throw to home plate.

7   In 2001, for example, the Yankees faced the Oakland A's in the playoffs. The Yankees lost the first two games. One more loss and their season would be over. In the third game, Jeter made a play that started a comeback by the Yankees. As Oakland's Jeremy Giambi headed for home, a Yankees outfielder made a weak throw toward the plate. Jeter dashed across the field and caught the ball. He then turned and made a perfect toss to the plate. Giambi was out. The Yankees went on to win the game. They also won the next two games, knocking Oakland out of the playoffs.

Skill Break
Sequence
Look at paragraph 4 on page 14.
Jeter joined the Yankees full-time in 1996. What happened next?

8   Baseball is only half of Derek Jeter's story, however. He is also a star off the field. For that he can thank his father, Charles, and his mother, Dorothy. They didn't let him get into any trouble growing up. His sister, Sharlee, said, "He had a lot of friends who could do whatever they wanted." But every year Jeter's parents made Derek and his sister sign a handwritten **contract.** It laid down the law. They had to study daily. They had to try their best to get A's in school. They had to do chores around the house. They had to be home early every night. And, there was no question about this, they had to agree not to drink or use drugs.

9   When Jeter was a boy, his hero was Yankees outfielder Dave Winfield. Jeter loved the way Winfield played, but he also admired Winfield for setting up his own **charity.** "He was my hero," said Jeter. "He went out of his way to help others." Jeter told himself that if he ever became a player in the major leagues, he would do the same thing.

10   Jeter kept that promise. In 1996 he set up his Turn 2 Foundation. The name comes from the baseball term for making a double play. In addition, 2 is Jeter's uniform number. Jeter hopes that troubled kids will "turn" to him and his foundation for help.

11   Turn 2 programs help city kids get off to a good start in life. They do this by teaching young people leadership skills and good study habits. Turn 2 programs guide kids away from drugs and alcohol. They also teach kids to eat right and to enjoy sports.

Fun Facts

▶ Jeter's favorite subject in school was math.

▶ He has a small role in the movie *Anger Management.*

▶ He has written two books: *The Life You Imagine* and *Game Day.*

Derek Jeter practices in Yankee Stadium before a game against the Baltimore Orioles.

12   Jeter's father, mother, and sister help run Turn 2. "I wanted it to have some meaning," says Jeter. "I wanted it to be something the family could do together. And it had to be hands-on. I didn't just want to give money. I wanted to be involved."

13   "I'm proud that Derek has taken it upon himself to do something like this," says Charles Jeter. "He's concerned about young people because when they fail, so much **potential** is destroyed."

14   "We are reaching a lot of kids," adds Derek Jeter, "and I am very proud of it."

15   In 2002 *Sporting News* gave Jeter a new honor. The magazine named him Number-One Good Guy in pro sports.

16   All baseball fans, of course, have their favorite team. That means most baseball fans across the country root against the New York Yankees. That's fair enough. The fans in Boston or Chicago or Detroit may not like the Yankees. But they have a hard time not liking Derek Jeter.

A Understanding What You Read

◆ **Fill in the circle next to each correct answer.**

1. In 1992 Jeter made a decision about whether he wanted to

○ A. play baseball in college or turn professional right away.

○ B. start in the major leagues or go to the minors first.

○ C. play for the Yankees or play for the Red Sox.

2. Which of the following statements is an opinion rather than a fact?

○ A. Jeter grew up in Michigan.

○ B. Jeter was named Rookie of the Year.

○ C. Jeter is the best all-around player.

3. When Jeter was a boy, who was his hero?

○ A. Charles Jeter

○ B. Dave Winfield

○ C. Paul O'Neill

4. Which sentence **best** states the main idea of the article?

○ A. Jeter created the Turn 2 Foundation in 1996.

○ B. Jeter is a well-known athlete from Michigan.

○ C. Jeter does great things in baseball and in the world.

5. The author probably wrote this article in order to

○ A. tell the reader about a famous baseball player.

○ B. entertain the reader with a funny baseball story.

○ C. make the reader think that the Yankees are great.

_____ Number of Correct Answers: Part A

B Finding the Sequence

◆ Read the paragraph below. It shows a sequence. Number the sentences below the paragraph to show the order of what happened.

1.

In 2001, for example, the Yankees faced the Oakland A's in the playoffs. The Yankees lost the first two games. One more loss and their season would be over. In the third game, Jeter made a play that started a comeback by the Yankees. As Oakland's Jeremy Giambi headed for home, a Yankees outfielder made a weak throw toward the plate. Jeter dashed across the field and caught the ball. He then turned and made a perfect toss to the plate. Giambi was out. The Yankees went on to win the game. They also won the next two games, knocking Oakland out of the playoffs.

_____ Jeter made a play that started a comeback by the Yankees.

_____ The Yankees and the A's both got into the playoffs.

_____ The Yankees won the third game.

_____ The Yankees lost two games in a row.

_____ The Yankees knocked the A's out of the playoffs.

◆ Reread paragraph 3 in the article. In Jeter's first season in the minor leagues, he hit just .202. Write what happened next.

2. _____

_____

_____ Number of Correct Answers: Part B

C Using Words

◆ The words and phrases in the list below relate to the words in the box. Some words or phrases in the list have a meaning that is the same as or similar to a word in the box. Some have the opposite meaning. Write the related word from the box on each line. Use each word from the box two times.

drafted	contract	potential
rookie	charity	

Same or similar meaning

1. future ability _____

2. deal _____

3. new guy _____

4. relief effort _____

5. promise _____

6. helpful giving _____

7. possible growth _____

8. called to join _____

Opposite meaning

9. not chosen _____

10. experienced player _____

_____ Number of Correct Answers: Part C

Writing About It

Write an Advertisement

◆ Suppose Derek Jeter is coming to visit your school. Use what you learned in the article to write an advertisement telling students about Jeter's visit. Use the checklist on page 103 to check your work.

Meet Derek Jeter at Our School!

The famous baseball player Derek Jeter will visit our school

next week. Jeter plays _____

_____.

He will talk about the importance of _____

_____.

He will also talk about his Turn 2 Foundaton. Turn 2 is _____

_____.

Lesson 2 Add your correct answers from parts A, B, and C to get your total score. Then find the percentage for your total score on the chart below. Record your percentage on the graph on page 105.

_____ Total Score for Parts A, B, and C

_____ Percentage

Total Score	1	2	3	4	5	6	7	8	9	10	11	12	13	14	15	16	17
Percentage	6	12	18	24	29	35	41	47	53	59	65	71	76	82	88	94	100

Lucy Liu

Shy Kid Becomes Hollywood Star

Birth Name Lucy Alexis Liu

Birth Date and Place December 2, 1968, Jackson Heights, Queens, New York

Home Los Angeles, California

Think About What You Know

Have you ever felt as if you didn't fit in with the other kids? Read the article to find out how Lucy Liu went from shy kid to successful actor.

Word Power

What do the words below tell you about the article?

wallflower a person who stands alone at parties or group events

culture the beliefs and abilities of a group of people, passed along from one generation to the next

sweatshop a place where people work long hours under bad conditions

martial art a type of fighting and self-defense, such as karate

embrace to honor and appreciate

Reading Skill

Author's Viewpoint An author's own feelings and beliefs are often shown in his or her writing. These feelings and beliefs are called the **author's viewpoint.** You can find clues about the author's viewpoint by paying attention to the author's choice of words.

Example

The people who move to the United States from other countries have much to offer. They strengthen the nation's workforce. A good example of this happened in the 1860s. That's when the first railroads that linked the West and East Coasts were built. Many of the workers who did this dangerous work were from China.

In this paragraph, the author talks about people who move to the United States from other countries. The author's viewpoint is that *this is a good thing.* One clue in the author's writing is the phrase "much to offer." What are some other clue phrases?

Lucy Liu
Shy Kid Becomes Hollywood Star

As a child, Lucy Liu didn't think she was very pretty. "The popular girls were all blond," she recalls. Liu, on the other hand, was a skinny Asian American kid with straight black hair. "I didn't have the blond, flipped hair or the curves," she says. But Liu couldn't feel bad about her looks forever. In 1999 she was named one of *People* magazine's "50 Most Beautiful People."

2   Lucy Liu was born and raised in a rough section of New York City. She was the youngest of three children born to Tom and Cecilia Liu. Her parents had come here from China. Back in their home country, they had both held good jobs. But in the United States they had to start all over again. Liu's mother worked as a clerk in a store. Her father picked up odd jobs wherever he could. The family barely had enough money to survive. They lived in an old apartment. She was often left alone while her parents worked. Lucy remembers the wallpaper that peeled off the walls. She remembers putting on boots and gloves and trying to kill the cockroaches that ran around her home. Most of all, she remembers the hunger.

3   "We were so poor we were lucky to have food at all," says Liu. "If we ate, it was boiled rice and boiled cucumber." Because of that, she says, "To this day I'll eat whatever is put in front of me."

4   Liu often felt uncomfortable at school. "I was such a shy kid," she recalls. "I would disappear into the background." She was, she says, "a total **wallflower.**" Part of the reason was her appearance. "My mother used to cut my hair really short," Liu says. "I think she used a tea saucer, not a bowl!"

5   But looks weren't Liu's only problem. She felt out of step with the other kids. "If your parents are not from America, you're basically living a different **culture,** with a different set of rules, at home," she says. For instance, Liu spoke English. But she also spoke Mandarin Chinese. "You go through a period when you don't like being Asian," she says. "You want to be 'American.'"

6   And then there was the money problem. To help the family get by, Liu's parents needed her to work. When she was 14, they found her and her brother jobs at a pajama factory. The conditions were terrible. It was a **sweatshop.** "I didn't want to do it, but what choice did we have?" Liu says.

7   Liu began to see that there was only one way for her to improve her life, and that was through education. She graduated from high school in 1986 and entered New York University. But Liu did not feel she had much in common with the other students. So she switched to the University of Michigan, where she began to study Asian languages and culture. She felt happier there. She says, "I started learning about myself and feeling good about life."

8   It was at the University of Michigan that Liu discovered acting. In her senior year, students were putting on the play *Alice in Wonderland*. Liu decided to try out for a part. She couldn't believe what happened. The lead role of Alice is usually played by someone with blond hair and blue eyes. But this time, the role of Alice went to Liu!

Skill Break
Author's Viewpoint
In paragraphs 1 through 5, the author introduces Lucy Liu and writes about her childhood.

What is the **author's viewpoint** about Liu's childhood?

What phrases did you use as clues?

9   Liu quickly found out that she loved being on stage. "I discovered a piece of me that had been missing all my life," she says. "It's almost like you miss a couple of chapters in a book, and something's not making sense, but you keep reading anyway. Then suddenly there are the missing chapters, and it all makes sense."

10   When Liu finished college, she wanted to keep acting. Her parents were not thrilled, but Liu insisted. She moved to California and began going to auditions. She hoped that someday she would make a living as an actor, but in the meantime, she needed money. So Liu did all sorts of jobs. She taught dance classes and cooked breakfasts for film crews. Says Liu, "They weren't great jobs, but I did them." To her, there was nothing unusual about this. "If you need a job, go . . . get a job," she says simply. "Work. That's the way I grew up."

11   In her spare time, Liu did many other things. She played the accordion. She did a kind of **martial art** called Kali-Eskrima-Silat. It involves fighting with sticks and knives. She also made her own art. She used all sorts of materials in her creations. She used rice paper, toys, and even trash. "Art really helps sometimes," Liu says. For her, it was a good way to relax. "It's better than going crazy," she says. In 1993 Liu showed her artwork at a New York art gallery. She even won a grant to study art in China.

Fun Facts

▶ Liu likes skiing, rock climbing, and horseback riding.

▶ She likes to buy and wear used clothing.

▶ She accidentally set herself on fire while filming *Charlie's Angels*.

Lucy Liu had to do a number of martial arts fight scenes for her role in *Charlie's Angels*.

12   Still, even with all these other interests, it was acting that Liu loved most. Throughout the 1990s, she kept going to auditions. At each one, she hoped to get lucky and win a big part. Instead her success came slowly. She played a few small parts on TV shows. Finally, in 1998, she got a bigger role. She began playing a lawyer on the TV show *Ally McBeal*. That's when Liu's acting career finally took off. In 2001 she starred as one of the three main characters in the movie *Charlie's Angels*. She also starred in the sequel, *Charlie's Angels: Full Throttle* (2003).

13   Lucy Liu has come a long way from the days of being the shy kid with a bad haircut. She's now a Hollywood star. And she hopes things will stay that way for years to come. "It's nice to be recognized," she says. Besides, she enjoys the challenge of acting, just as she enjoys all the other things she does. As she puts it, "I want to **embrace** life as long as I have it."

A Understanding What You Read

◆ Fill in the circle next to each correct answer for questions 1, 2, and 5. Follow the directions shown for questions 3 and 4.

1. Liu went to work in a pajama factory because

○ A. her first acting jobs didn't pay much.

○ B. her family needed more money.

○ C. she was saving to go to college.

2. What did Liu decide she needed to do to improve her life?

○ A. get a good education

○ B. earn a grant to study in China

○ C. move to California

3. In which paragraph did you find the information to answer question 2? Write the paragraph number on the line.

_____

4. Choose from the letters below to correctly complete the following statement. Write the letters on the lines.

On the negative side, _____, but on the positive side, _____.

A. Liu found a satisfying career in acting

B. Liu could not speak English at school

C. Liu had a difficult childhood

5. From the information in the article, you can predict that Liu will

○ A. become a professional artist.

○ B. get acting roles in more movies.

○ C. move back to New York.

_____ Number of Correct Answers: Part A

B Finding the Author's Viewpoint

◆ Read the paragraph below. Fill in the circle next to the sentence that **best** describes the author's viewpoint about Liu's acting career.

1.

Lucy Liu has come a long way from the days of being the shy kid with a bad haircut. She's now a Hollywood star. And she hopes things will stay that way for years to come. "It's nice to be recognized," she says. Besides, she enjoys the challenge of acting, just as she enjoys all the other things she does. As she puts it, "I want to embrace life as long as I have it."

○ A. Liu has found a good life as an actor.
○ B. Liu should try a different career.
○ C. Liu enjoys other things more than acting.

◆ What clues helped you find the author's viewpoint? Write **three** clues on the lines below.

2. _____

_____

_____

_____ Number of Correct Answers: Part B

C Using Words

◆ Cross out one of the four words in each row that does not relate to the word or phrase in dark type.

1. wallflower

shy   timid   tall   quiet

2. culture

food   clouds   language   beliefs

3. sweatshop

work   healthy   hard   tired

4. martial art

strength   protect   practice   laugh

5. embrace

walk   enjoy   welcome   love

◆ Choose one of the words shown above in dark type. Write a sentence using the word.

6. word: _____

_____

_____

_____ Number of Correct Answers: Part C

D   Writing About It

Write a Magazine Article

◆ Suppose you are a writer for a movie magazine. Use what you learned about Lucy Liu to write a magazine article about her. Finish the sentences below to write your article. Use the checklist on page 103 to check your work.

Lucy Liu is one of today's big Hollywood stars. She discovered

acting when _____

_____.

In her first big TV role, she _____

_____.

You may have seen her starring in the movies _____

_____.

Stay tuned for more from Lucy Liu!

Lesson 3 Add your correct answers from parts A, B, and C to get your total score. Then find the percentage for your total score on the chart below. Record your percentage on the graph on page 105.

_____ Total Score for Parts A, B, and C

_____ Percentage

Total Score	1	2	3	4	5	6	7	8	9	10	11	12	13
Percentage	8	15	23	31	38	46	54	62	69	77	85	92	100

Compare and Contrast

◆ Think about the celebrities, or famous people, in Unit One. Pick two articles that tell about celebrities who have talents and interests beyond their main careers. Use information from the articles to fill in this chart.

Celebrity's Name		
What is the celebrity's main career?		
What are the celebrity's other talents or interests?		
How does the celebrity use these other talents or interests?		

Salma Hayek

Petra Nemcova

Lance Armstrong

Salma Hayek
Proving Herself

Birth Name Salma Hayek Jimenez
Birth Date and Place September 2, 1968, Coatzacoalcos, Veracruz, Mexico
Home Hollywood, California

Think About What You Know

Have you ever doubted yourself? Did it make you try harder? Read the article to find out what Salma Hayek did to prove her abilities.

Word Power

What do the words below tell you about the article?

gymnastics physical exercises that develop strength and balance

chauffeur a person who works as a driver

naive lacking knowledge about the way things work in the world

guild an association of people with similar interests or goals

funding a sum of money used for a specific purpose

Reading Skill

Main Idea and Supporting Details The **main idea** gives a paragraph its purpose and direction. The paragraph's **details** support and explain the main idea. There may be many details in a paragraph but only one main idea. The supporting details are specific ideas. The main idea is a more general idea.

Example

Main Idea	Frida Kahlo was a Mexican painter who had a unique style. She lived from 1907 to 1954. Her paintings were
Supporting Details	very different from the paintings of other artists. She once said, "I put on the canvas whatever comes into my mind."

"Frida Kahlo was a Mexican painter who had a unique style" is the main idea. What are the three supporting details?

Salma Hayek

Proving Herself

When Salma Hayek was eight years old, she wanted **gymnastics** lessons. So her father signed her up. But he didn't take Hayek to just any gym. He took her to the best gymnastics school in all of Mexico City.

2   That's pretty much the way things were for Hayek throughout her childhood. Hayek's father was a rich Lebanese business owner, and her mother was a Mexican opera singer. Both of them wanted their daughter to have the best of everything. They gave her a beautiful pink bedroom in their home in Veracruz, Mexico. They gave her lots of fancy clothes. When she wanted pets, they let her have monkeys and even a tiger. When she asked to go to school in the United States, they sent her to a Louisiana boarding school for a couple of years. And when other teenagers were learning to drive, Hayek didn't bother because her **chauffeur** took her everywhere.

3   While Hayek's parents were giving her everything that money could buy, her grandmother was focusing on Hayek's looks. Again and again, the grandmother shaved baby Salma's head, believing this would make the little girl's hair grow in thicker and more beautiful. She clipped Hayek's eyebrows for the same reason.

4   As Hayek grew older, the shavings stopped, but the entire family continued to treat her like royalty. Her father even called her *"mi princesa,"* or "my princess." Hayek, however, says that she was "a spoiled brat." Still, the way she was raised did teach her one important thing. It made her believe she could do anything. So when she decided to become an actor, no one could change her mind.

5   Hayek began her acting career in a local theater when she was 20 years old. She followed this up with several TV commercials. Then, in 1989, she got a lead role in a Mexican soap opera. By the following year, at age 22, she was one of the biggest TV stars in all of Mexico.

6   It seemed that Salma Hayek had it all. She had wealth, beauty, and fame. Her parents were delighted, but Hayek herself wasn't satisfied. As she puts it, "I kept thinking, 'I'm famous, but am I good?'" She didn't think she would ever be able to answer that question if she stayed in Mexico. The only place to prove herself as an actor, she concluded, was the United States. So, in 1991, she packed two suitcases and left for California.

7   Hayek thought she would soon rule Hollywood the way she ruled everything else in her life, but she quickly discovered she was wrong. First of all, she didn't speak much English. It had been 10 years since she'd left the boarding school in Louisiana, and during that time she had forgotten most of the English she'd learned. "I thought I'd pick up the language again in three months," she recalls. "Then I came here and realized . . . it wasn't going to be hard to learn. It was going to be nearly impossible."

8   Hayek had other problems as well. "I didn't have a green card," she says, referring to the card that allows people from other countries to work in this country. "I didn't know I had to have an agent, I couldn't drive . . . I was so **naive.**"

Skill Break
Main Idea and Supporting Details
Look at paragraph 7 on this page. In this paragraph the author explains what happened when Hayek arrived in Hollywood.

What is the **main idea** of the paragraph?

What **details** support the main idea?

9   Over the next couple of years, Hayek solved these problems. She took English lessons and learned to drive a car. She sent videotapes of her work to agents, hoping one would respond. "I knocked on many doors and got turned down many times," she recalls. Finally, she got a small part, with just one line, in the movie *Mi Vida Loca* (1994). That allowed her to join the Screen Actors **Guild.** At last, she thought, she was ready to become a Hollywood star.

10   Once again, Hayek was wrong. It turned out that Hollywood didn't have much use for Mexican actresses. "There were no parts for Latinas," she recalls. She was given a few minor roles playing maids or waitresses. But that was it. "It was very painful," says Hayek. "People close to me advised me to go back to Mexico, settle down, and have kids. I think that they felt sorry for me."

11   Fortunately, in 1995, Hayek appeared on a late-night cable talk show. A director named Robert Rodriguez happened to be watching. Rodriguez was impressed by Hayek's good looks and strong personality. And he liked what she had to say. "American films don't usually have leading roles for Latin women," she said on the show. "But I intend to change that." Rodriguez believed that Hayek had star quality. He contacted her and asked her to costar with Antonio Banderas in *Desperado*. Hayek quickly accepted the opportunity.

▶ Hayek has two dogs, which she found on the streets of Mexico City.

▶ Her first name means "peace" in Arabic.

▶ She likes basketball, and her favorite team is the Los Angeles Lakers.

Salma Hayek plays Mexican painter Frida Kahlo.

12   Hayek went on to make other movies with big-name stars. She made *From Dusk Till Dawn* (1996) with George Clooney and *Breaking Up* (1997) with Russell Crowe. She made movies with Matthew Perry, Ben Affleck, and Matt Damon. Still, Hayek was not happy with her career. She wanted to make a movie with serious roles for Latin women. Finally, she says, "I got sick of listening to myself and decided to . . . try to do something."

13   What Hayek did was make an incredible movie. That movie is *Frida,* based on the story of Mexican painter Frida Kahlo. Hayek plays the lead role in the movie and is also the producer. It took her years to get the movie made. She had to get **funding.** She had to get film rights to the story. And she had to find good people to costar in it. When the movie finally came out in 2002, it got great reviews. It earned Hayek the Golden Globe Award for Best Actress.

14   Salma Hayek had done it. She had shown the world, and herself, just how talented she was. "For 18 years I have worked really hard to improve myself and have fought to earn some respectability as an actress," she told a reporter in 2003. "Now I wake up in the morning with a smile on my face."

◆ **Fill in the circle next to each correct answer.**

1. Hayek didn't learn to drive as a teenager because she

○ A. was afraid of getting in an accident.

○ B. couldn't speak English very well.

○ C. had a driver to take her everywhere.

2. Which of the following statements is an opinion rather than a fact?

○ A. She had to get the film rights.

○ B. I think they felt sorry for me.

○ C. I didn't have a green card.

3. Hayek made the movie *Frida* because she wanted to

○ A. create serious movie roles for Latin women.

○ B. star in a big movie with Antonio Banderas.

○ C. be able to join the Screen Actors Guild.

4. From Hayek's actions, you can conclude that she

○ A. never learned to speak English very well.

○ B. has the will to work hard to get what she wants.

○ C. sees being a famous actress as her lifelong goal.

5. The author probably wrote this article in order to

○ A. inform the reader about Hayek's career.

○ B. persuade the reader to see Hayek's movies.

○ C. entertain the reader with a funny Hollywood story.

_____ Number of Correct Answers: Part A

B Finding the Main Idea and Supporting Details

◆ Read the paragraph below. Fill in the circle next to the sentence that is the **best** main idea for the paragraph.

1.

Over the next couple of years, Hayek solved these problems. She took English lessons and learned to drive a car. She sent videotapes of her work to agents, hoping one would respond. "I knocked on many doors and got turned down many times," she recalls. Finally, she got a small part, with just one line, in the movie *Mi Vida Loca* (1994). That allowed her to join the Screen Actors Guild. At last, she thought, she was ready to become a Hollywood star.

○ A. At last, she thought, she was ready to become a Hollywood star.
○ B. She got a small part, with just one line, in the movie *Mi Vida Loca.*
○ C. Over the next couple of years, Hayek solved these problems.

◆ Reread paragraph 13 in the article. Write the main idea and at least **two** supporting details.

2. Main Idea: _____

Supporting Details: _____

_____

_____

_____

_____ Number of Correct Answers: Part B

C Using Words

Complete each sentence with a word from the box. Write the missing word on the line.

gymnastics	naive	funding
chauffeur	guild	

1. The people in the poetry _____ meet once a month to share their poems.

2. The _____ drove us to the airport.

3. I learned how to flip and then land without falling in my

_____ class.

4. They decided he was too _____ to travel alone.

5. We need to find the necessary _____ to build a new library.

Choose one word from the box. Write a new sentence using the word.

6. word: _____

_____

_____

_____ Number of Correct Answers: Part C

42

D Writing About It

Write Your Thoughts

◆ Finish the sentences below. Use the checklist on page 103 to check your work.

I wonder why Salma Hayek _____

_____.

Maybe it's because _____

_____.

How Did You Do?

◆ Finish the sentence below. Use the checklist on page 103 to check your work.

From reading this article, I have learned _____

_____

_____.

Lesson 4 Add your correct answers from parts A, B, and C to get your total score. Then find the percentage for your total score on the chart below. Record your percentage on the graph on page 105.

_____ Total Score for Parts A, B, and C

_____ Percentage

Total Score	1	2	3	4	5	6	7	8	9	10	11	12	13
Percentage	8	15	23	31	38	46	54	62	69	77	85	92	100

Petra Nemcova

A Second Chance at Life

Birth Name Petra Nemcova

Birth Date and Place June 24, 1979, Karviná, Czechoslovakia

Homes New York City and London, England

Think About What You Know

What is the most dangerous situation you have ever been in? What did you do? Read the article to find out what Petra Nemcova did when she was in great danger.

Word Power

What do the words below tell you about the article?

edition a particular issue of a book or magazine

unimaginable impossible to picture or think about

tsunami a huge ocean wave caused by an underwater earthquake

bungalow a small house

pelvis the bones that support and protect the area of the lower stomach

Reading Skill

Sequence The order of events in a story or an article is called **sequence.** The author will not always use signal words such as *first* and *then*. Sometimes you must use what you know and clues from the text to find the sequence.

Example

The First Event   He bought his first camera when he was in college at the University of Iowa. When he was

The Next Event   working in New York, he began taking pictures of interesting people.

"He bought his first camera" is the first event in the sequence. The second event is "he began taking pictures of interesting people." How might you use the clues in the text and what you already know to find this sequence?

Petra Nemcova

A Second Chance at Life

It had been a very busy year for Petra Nemcova. The 25-year-old supermodel had flown all over the world, doing one modeling job after another. Finally, in December 2004, she was ready for a vacation. She wanted a couple of weeks just to relax and unwind. So she made reservations at the Thailand beach resort of Khao Lak. Here, Nemcova expected to find plenty of sun, sand, and warm ocean water. She had no way of knowing that she would soon find herself in the middle of one of the worst natural disasters in modern history.

2   Nemcova grew up in Czechoslovakia (now the Czech Republic). As a young girl, she was "really, really shy." But when she was a teenager, a friend convinced her to talk to a talent agent. The agent quickly started Nemcova on a modeling career. In 2003, at the age of 23, Nemcova appeared on the cover of *Sports Illustrated*'s swimsuit **edition.** That quickly brought her international fame. Suddenly everyone wanted her for advertisements, fashion shows, and magazine covers. A TV network made plans for her to star in a show about modeling. And photographs were taken for a 2005 Petra Nemcova calendar.

3   At the end of 2004, in the midst of all this excitement, Nemcova took off for Khao Lak. With her went photographer Simon Atlee, her boyfriend of two years. Atlee was the one who had taken the photos for Nemcova's upcoming calendar. He, too, had had a busy year, and Nemcova knew he would enjoy a vacation as much as she would.

4   Nemcova and Atlee settled into Khao Lak, and for the first few days they did have a wonderful time. But on December 26, something **unimaginable** happened. An earthquake struck deep in the Indian Ocean, sending a mammoth wave rushing toward land. This wave, called a **tsunami,** hit Indonesia and Sri Lanka. It hit India. It even reached the east coast of Africa. A wall of water up to 100 feet high destroyed almost everything in its path. Over 200,000 people died in this natural disaster.

5   The tsunami hit Thailand's beaches with great force. It hit Khao Lak, where Nemcova and Atlee were relaxing in a **bungalow.** All of a sudden, water came pouring in around them. "I heard people screaming, and I looked out the window," recalls Nemcova. "The water was coming in, coming in, and Simon was just saying, 'Petra, Petra, what's going on?'"

6   Nemcova called out to Atlee, suggesting that they should climb onto the roof. But there was no time. And the roof wouldn't have been high enough anyway. In the next instant, the wave struck with full force. Says Nemcova, "In a split second it pulled us out of the bungalow."

7   Nemcova found herself swallowed up by a swirling, pounding current of water. "At that moment the power of the water was carrying fallen trees, broken buildings," she recalls. It was too strong to fight, too strong to swim through. As she says, "You couldn't do anything. You just had to go with it."

Skill Break

Sequence

Look at paragraph 6 on this page. In this paragraph, the author describes what happened to Nemcova and Atlee when the tsunami first struck.

Nemcova suggested that they climb onto the roof to avoid the water. What happened next?

8   Desperate to get to safety, Nemcova spotted a small island of debris sticking out of the water. Thinking it might be solid, she put her feet out and tried to stand on it. But the pile crumbled, sucking her legs in among the boards, branches, and foaming water.

9   Then Nemcova heard Atlee calling her name. "Petra! Petra!" he cried. It was the last time she would ever hear his voice. A moment later, he was gone. And a moment after that, a large uprooted tree struck Nemcova. It hit her in the middle of her body, shattering all six bones in her **pelvis.**

10   With pain flooding her body and water washing over her head, she thought surely she would die. But a few seconds later she bobbed to the surface and managed to take a gulp of air. She saw the top of a palm tree and reached for it. She missed. "Then there was another one," she says. "I didn't see any more of them, so that was my chance."

11   She grabbed hold of this second treetop and held on with all her might. The raging water kept driving her left hip into the trunk of the tree, causing her terrible pain, but still she hung on.

12   "I was just screaming from the top of my lungs," she recalls. And she wasn't the only one. All around her, men, women, and children were crying out for help. She heard them, but there was nothing she could do. "I just tried to survive," she says, "and tried to think positive."

Fun Facts

▶ As a child, Nemcova liked to pick blueberries in the mountains around her town.

▶ She did not watch TV until she was 10 years old.

▶ She greets people by giving them three kisses on the cheeks.

Petra Nemcova and Simon Atlee pose together in France seven months before their trip to Thailand.

13   For the next seven and a half hours, Nemcova clung to that tree. At last, as the water level started to drop, a group of rescuers came by and helped her down. "I was so broken, I couldn't walk," she says. "There were so many people with horrible injuries, with blood everywhere. It was like a war movie."

14   Nemcova spent two weeks in a hospital in Thailand and then was transferred to a hospital in the Czech Republic, where much of her family lives. Doctors are amazed by what she has been through. "I do not know how she survived," says one.

15   Nemcova knows she is lucky to be alive. Eventually her injuries will heal, and she will be able to return to modeling. But she isn't sure she wants to be a supermodel anymore. "I'm different now," she says, "with a completely different view of the world." She still mourns Simon Atlee, whose body was found two months after the tsunami. "I lost the person closest to me," she points out. "And I got a second chance to live. So, in a way, I feel that I live for both of us." Whatever she decides to do in the future, Nemcova wants to make the most of that life.

A Understanding What You Read

◆ **Fill in the circle next to each correct answer.**

1. Which is the best description of Nemcova as a young girl?

   ○ A. She was a good swimmer.
   ○ B. She was very shy.
   ○ C. She had many friends.

2. From what you read, which of these is probably true?

   ○ A. Nemcova was one of the oldest tsunami victims.
   ○ B. Nemcova was one of the weakest tsunami victims.
   ○ C. Nemcova was one of the most famous tsunami victims.

3. When Nemcova realized the tsunami was coming, her first idea was to

   ○ A. climb onto the bungalow's roof.
   ○ B. stand on an island of debris.
   ○ C. hold on to the top of a tree.

4. From the information in the article, you can predict that Nemcova will

   ○ A. move to a bungalow in Thailand.
   ○ B. miss Simon Atlee for a long time.
   ○ C. quickly return to modeling.

5. What lesson about life does this story teach?

   ○ A. Some experiences change a person forever.
   ○ B. Danger can be waiting around every corner.
   ○ C. It's usually best to vacation close to home.

_____ Number of Correct Answers: Part A

B Finding the Sequence

◆ Read the paragraph below. It shows a sequence. Number the sentences below the paragraph to show the order of what happened.

1.

    Nemcova grew up in Czechoslovakia (now the Czech Republic). As a young girl, she was "really, really shy." But when she was a teenager, a friend convinced her to talk to a talent agent. The agent quickly started Nemcova on a modeling career. In 2003, at the age of 23, Nemcova appeared on the cover of *Sports Illustrated's* swimsuit edition. That quickly brought her international fame. Suddenly everyone wanted her for advertisements, fashion shows, and magazine covers. A TV network made plans for her to star in a show about modeling. And photographs were taken for a 2005 Petra Nemcova calendar.

_____ The agent started Nemcova on a modeling career.

_____ Photographs were taken for a 2005 Petra Nemcova calendar.

_____ Nemcova became internationally famous.

_____ Nemcova appeared on the cover of *Sports Illustrated*.

_____ A friend convinced her to talk to a talent agent.

◆ Reread paragraph 14 in the article. Nemcova spent two weeks in a hospital in Thailand. Write what happened next.

2. _____

_____ Number of Correct Answers: Part B

C Using Words

◆ The words in the list below relate to the words in the box. Some words in the list have a meaning that is the same as or similar to a word in the box. Some have the opposite meaning. Write the related word from the box on each line. Use each word from the box two times.

edition	tsunami	pelvis
unimaginable	bungalow	

Same or similar meaning

1. bones _____

2. publication _____

3. shocking _____

4. wave _____

5. cottage _____

6. flood _____

7. issue _____

8. hips _____

Opposite meaning

9. expected _____

10. palace _____

_____ Number of Correct Answers: Part C

52

D Writing About It

Write a Story

◆ Write a story about Petra Nemcova's life. Finish the sentences below to write your story. Use the checklist on page 103 to check your work.

Petra Nemcova grew up in Czechoslovakia. A talent agent helped

her _____.

She had a terrifying experience when _____

_____.

Her boyfriend, Simon Atlee, _____

_____.

Grateful to be alive, Nemcova wants to _____

_____.

Lesson 5 Add your correct answers from parts A, B, and C to get your total score. Then find the percentage for your total score on the chart below. Record your percentage on the graph on page 105.

_____ Total Score for Parts A, B, and C

_____ Percentage

Total Score	1	2	3	4	5	6	7	8	9	10	11	12	13	14	15	16	17
Percentage	6	12	18	24	29	35	41	47	53	59	65	71	76	82	88	94	100

Lance Armstrong

Living Strong

Birth Name Lance Edward Gunderson

Birth Date and Place September 18, 1971, Plano, Texas

Home Austin, Texas

Think About What You Know

Is there someone who inspires you? What has this person done to inspire you? Read the article to find out why Lance Armstrong inspires people throughout the world.

Word Power

What do the words below tell you about the article?

cyclist someone who rides a bicycle

miraculous amazing or extraordinary

mentality way of thinking or outlook

grueling very difficult or exhausting

dominated had the most power and was able to control

Reading Skill

Author's Viewpoint An author's own feelings and beliefs are often shown in his or her writing. These feelings and beliefs are called the **author's viewpoint.** You can find clues about the author's viewpoint by paying attention to the author's choice of words.

Example

> Exercise can be a powerful tool to fight disease. First, exercise reduces your stress level. High stress makes you more likely to get sick. Also, exercise increases the oxygen level in your body. Oxygen plays a key role in building your body's ability to fight disease. Exercising regularly is a smart choice.

In this paragraph, the author talks about exercise and staying well. The author's viewpoint is that *exercise is good for your health.* One clue in the author's writing is the phrase "a powerful tool." What are some other clue phrases?

Lance Armstrong

Living Strong

His doctors gave him less than a 50-50 chance to live. So who would have predicted that Lance Armstrong would not only live but would go on to become the best **cyclist** in history? The odds against him doing that must have been a million to one. Yet that's exactly what Armstrong did. "It is absolutely **miraculous,**" says James Reeves, one of Armstrong's doctors.

2   In 1996 the 25-year-old Armstrong learned that he had cancer. At the time, he was one of the top cyclists in the world. He had already won every major road race in the United States. In 1993 he had won the 160-mile World Cycling Championship in Norway. Armstrong had won despite rain, slippery roads, and two crashes. He had raced in the Tour de France, the most famous bicycle race in the world.

3   But in the fall of 1996, Armstrong learned that his career—and his very life—were in danger. Armstrong had not felt well for a while. At first he didn't think it was anything serious. After all, he was young and strong and reaching the height of his career. "I felt bulletproof," he recalls. Then one day he began to spit up blood. That scared him into going to the doctor. On October 3, the doctor gave Armstrong the bad news. He had cancer. And that wasn't all. The cancer had spread to his lungs, stomach, and even his brain. Naturally, Armstrong was terrified by the news. "It was the worst fear I'd ever experienced," he says.

4   But Armstrong refused to feel sorry for himself. On October 8, he declared, "I'm determined to fight this disease, and I will win. I intend to ride again as a pro cyclist."

5   The rest of the cycling world did not believe him. "After I got sick," recalls Armstrong, "the **mentality** in cycling was, 'He's finished, done, history.'" In fact, he was cut from his cycling team.

6   Armstrong had two operations to remove the cancer. He also had chemotherapy, which is treatment with powerful drugs that work to kill cancer cells. The treatments worked, and within a year Armstrong's doctors declared him cancer-free.

7   By the summer of 1997, Armstrong felt strong enough to travel to Europe to see some races. He also began riding again. He started slowly, going out for just an hour or so. But soon he began going longer and harder. By the fall, he began to think that he really could race again.

8   Armstrong returned to racing in the spring of 1998. He joined a new team, the U.S. Postal Service cycling team. He wasn't much of a threat at first, but soon his old strength returned. In the fall of 1998, he finished fourth in the Tour of Spain. He did well in other races too. George Hincapie, one of his teammates, marveled, "Lance was a strong rider before he got cancer, but he's even stronger now."

9   In 1999 Armstrong announced that he would compete in the Tour de France. This is one of the toughest sporting challenges in the world. It is a **grueling** test of courage and endurance. Cyclists race around France, sometimes briefly riding into a neighboring country, for three weeks. The exact roads used vary from year to year, but the total distance is usually about 2,200 miles.

Skill Break
Author's Viewpoint
Look at paragraph 1 on page 56. The author talks about how Lance Armstrong lived through a life-threatening situation.

What is the **author's viewpoint** about Armstrong's recovery?

What phrases did you use as clues?

10　　The Tour de France is really 20 or so daily races called "stages." Some of the stages go through the rolling French countryside. Others go over the mighty Alps. The cyclist who has the lowest total time for all the stages is the winner.

11　　To the surprise of almost everyone, Armstrong **dominated** the Tour. He won by 7 minutes and 37 seconds. It was the fastest time in Tour history. Armstrong became only the second American ever to win the Tour de France.

12　　That was just the beginning. Armstrong won the Tour de France each of the next three years. In 2003 Armstrong tried for his fifth straight victory, but this time he had some trouble. First, he came down with the flu just before the race began. Then, during stage 1, he got caught in a pileup when a biker ahead of him crashed. By the end of stage 8, Armstrong was in first place, but he did not have the kind of commanding lead that he had usually had in previous Tours.

13　　Slowly other cyclists began to catch up. During stage 12, Armstrong didn't get enough water. This slowed him down and cost him precious minutes. Then, during stage 15, he was riding so close to the edge of the road that his handlebars caught the strap of a fan's pocketbook. Armstrong lost control of his bike and fell to the ground.

14　　The shock of the fall seemed to spark something in him. He remembers thinking, "Lance, if you want to win the Tour de France, do it today." He jumped back on his bike and pedaled like mad. By the end of the day, he had regained control of the race, and he went on to win his fifth straight Tour de France.

Fun Facts

▶ Armstrong wrote the book *It's Not About the Bike: My Journey Back to Life.*

▶ He has three children.

▶ His heart is larger than the average human heart. It can beat as fast as 201 times per minute.

Lance Armstrong celebrates as he crosses the finish line to win his sixth straight Tour de France.

15   Armstrong raced in the Tour once again in 2004, and once again he won. This set an all-time record. Two other riders had won five times, but no one had won the race six times—much less six times in a row. But Armstrong wasn't finished. He made plans to race again in 2005, win his seventh straight Tour de France, and retire from the sporting world a champion, which is exactly what he did.

16   Lance Armstrong has proved himself to be a superior athlete. More than that, he has become an inspiration to people fighting cancer. As he puts it, "Before cancer, I just lived. Now I live strong." These words are echoed by the Lance Armstrong Foundation, which he started in 1997 to help other cancer patients. More than 40 million people around the globe wear the foundation's yellow "LIVESTRONG" bracelets to show their support for those living with cancer.

17   Armstrong is proud that his life story gives other people hope. As he says, "If there's one thing I say to those who use me as their example, it's that if you ever get a second chance in life, you've got to go all the way."

A Understanding What You Read

◆ **Fill in the circle next to each correct answer.**

1. Why did Armstrong decide to visit the doctor?

○ A. He got the flu before a race.
○ B. He was hurt in a cycling accident.
○ C. He began to spit up blood.

2. What did Armstrong do to recover from cancer?

○ A. He had two operations and chemotherapy.
○ B. He kept cycling and training for races.
○ C. He stayed at home and avoided the hospital.

3. From what the article told you about Armstrong's athletic achievements, you can conclude that

○ A. the world has yet to see what Armstrong can really do.
○ B. his wins would be remarkable even if he'd never had cancer.
○ C. few people today know about Armstrong's successes.

4. Which sentence **best** states the main idea of the article?

○ A. Armstrong thought he was healthy when he was very sick.
○ B. Armstrong beat cancer and became the world's top cyclist.
○ C. Armstrong won the Tour de France seven times in a row.

5. Which of the following categories would this story fit into?

○ A. Great Trips to France
○ B. Predictable Sports Stories
○ C. Amazing Recoveries

_____ Number of Correct Answers: Part A

B Finding the Author's Viewpoint

◆ Read the paragraph below. Fill in the circle next to the sentence that **best** describes the author's viewpoint about Armstrong's actions.

1.

Lance Armstrong has proved himself to be a superior athlete. More than that, he has become an inspiration to people fighting cancer. As he puts it, "Before cancer, I just lived. Now I live strong." These words are echoed by the Lance Armstrong Foundation, which he started in 1997 to help other cancer patients. More than 40 million people around the globe wear the foundation's yellow "LIVESTRONG" bracelets to show their support for those living with cancer.

○ A. Armstrong is better at competing in sports than at helping others.
○ B. Armstrong's greatest deed was to inspire people who have cancer.
○ C. Armstrong could have done more to help cancer patients.

◆ What clues helped you find the author's viewpoint?
Write **three** clues on the lines.

2. _____

_____

_____

_____ Number of Correct Answers: Part B

C Using Words

◆ Cross out one of the four words in each row that does not
relate to the word in dark type.

1. cyclist

wheels   picture   exercise   bike

2. miraculous

unusual   incredible   fancy   marvelous

3. mentality

sleep   ideas   attitude   thoughts

4. grueling

hard   tiring   painful   strange

5. dominated

winner   lead   comfort   strength

◆ Choose one of the words shown above in dark type. Write a
sentence using the word.

6. word: _____

_____

_____

_____ Number of Correct Answers: Part C

Write a Comic Strip

◆ Write a comic strip about Lance Armstrong. First look at what's happening in each scene. Then finish the sentence in each bubble. Use the checklist on page 103 to check your work.

Lesson 6 Add your correct answers from parts A, B, and C to get your total score. Then find the percentage for your total score on the chart below. Record your percentage on the graph on page 105.

_____ Total Score for Parts A, B, and C

_____ Percentage

Total Score	1	2	3	4	5	6	7	8	9	10	11	12	13
Percentage	8	15	23	31	38	46	54	62	69	77	85	92	100

Compare and Contrast

◆ Think about the celebrities, or famous people, in Unit Two. Pick two articles that tell about celebrities who experienced something that they did not expect. Use information from the articles to fill in this chart.

Celebrity's Name		
What happened that the celebrity was not expecting?		
What had the celebrity expected to happen?		
How did the celebrity respond to what happened?		

Clay Aiken

Veronica Campbell

Marc Anthony

Clay Aiken

Winning Big in Second Place

Birth Name Clayton Holmes Grissom

Birth Date and Place November 30, 1978, Chapel Hill, North Carolina

Home Los Angeles, California

Think About What You Know

Have you ever *not* won at something you tried for but felt happy anyway? Read the article to find out how Clay Aiken came in second place and still found much success.

Word Power

What do the words below tell you about the article?

disabilities conditions that limit someone's ability to do things

interacting doing things with others

flinch to quickly pull back due to fear or discomfort

unconditional not limited by anything

regional relating to a specific area or region

Reading Skill

Main Idea and Supporting Details The **main idea** of a paragraph is not always directly stated in the text. Sometimes you must look for clues about the main idea in the paragraph's **details.** You can study the individual details to find the main idea.

Example

Singers have to drink plenty of water. They also have to rest their voices. Since colds and sore throats can be harmful to their voices, singers also have to keep themselves healthy.

The main idea of this paragraph is that *singers have to take good care of their voices,* but it is not directly stated in the text. How can the reader find the main idea?

Clay Aiken

Winning Big in Second Place

You don't always have to win to be a winner. That's certainly the case with pop singer Clay Aiken. In 2003 Aiken finished second to Ruben Studdard on the TV talent show *American Idol.* But within five months of losing to Studdard, Aiken sold more albums than Studdard or any other *American Idol* finalist. No one guessed he would become a big star—least of all Aiken. "I did not expect to be here at all," he says.

2   Growing up in North Carolina, Aiken knew he could sing. "I've been singing forever," he says. He sang in local school productions and in the Raleigh Boys Choir. He even stood on carpet squares in the local department store, where his mother worked, and sang to customers. "Clay was always the entertainer," says his mother. "Give him anything that looked like a microphone, and he'd perform."

3   Yet Aiken never had any dreams of being a professional singer. At one point he wanted to be a reporter, and for a while he thought he might run for public office. In the end, however, he decided to become a teacher. Aiken went to the University of North Carolina to study special education. He dreamed of working with children who have learning **disabilities.** "I fell in love with working with the kids," he says.

4   While he was in college, Aiken got a job helping autistic children. People who are autistic have trouble communicating and **interacting** with others. Aiken began to work with an autistic boy named Mike Bubel. Says Mike's mother, Diane, "He cannot speak, and he can't always process what is said to him. You can't just tell him things like 'put your shoes on,' so it can be very difficult."

5   When faced with this tough challenge, Aiken didn't even **flinch.** Diane Bubel knows that working with an autistic child isn't easy. It takes patience and respect. Each child must be treated as an individual. That was how Aiken worked with 12-year-old Mike. "Clayton walked in the door with **unconditional** love and no expectations," says Diane. "It's rare to find people that open and understanding."

6   It was Diane Bubel and her family who pushed Aiken to audition for *American Idol*. When they heard him sing, they knew he had real talent. "We realized what an incredible voice he had and just kept telling him to audition for *American Idol,*" says Diane.

7   After much prodding, Aiken decided to give it a shot. "Fine," he said at last, "I'll do it if you just keep quiet."

8   Aiken auditioned at a **regional** tryout for *American Idol* in Charlotte, North Carolina, but the judges cut him. He could have stopped right there, but a voice inside of him said, "I think I'm better than that." So he went to a second regional audition in Atlanta, Georgia, where he stood in line with thousands of other hopeful candidates. "I was not expecting to make it through that line of 6,000, much less go to Hollywood," he says. This time, though, the judges saw something they liked about him.

Skill Break
Main Idea and Supporting Details
Look at paragraph 8 on this page. The paragraph gives details about Aiken's experience trying out for *American Idol*.

From the information in the **details,** what is the **main idea** of the paragraph?

9   He certainly didn't make a strong impression when he first walked onstage. He was tall and skinny, with funny glasses and a bad haircut. His shirt was not tucked in, and he was wearing big ugly shoes. People described him at this point as a "nerd" and a "geek." But his voice won over the judges. Said judge Simon Cowell, "You don't look like a pop star . . . but you've got a great voice."

10   Judge Randy Jackson agreed, saying, "Yeah, it's weird, it's wild . . . to hear that voice coming out of this . . ." Jackson didn't finish the sentence. He only said that Aiken should "work on his style." The judges then announced that he was "coming to Hollywood!"

11   Aiken had made it into the group of 32 finalists, but that was almost as far as he got. He was one of the first ones cut from that group. Luckily he was asked to come back for the "wild card show," which is designed to give one more chance to finalists who have been cut. From then on, Aiken's fate was decided by *American Idol* viewers.

12   Each week viewers voted for the performer they liked best, and the performer with the fewest votes was sent home. Every week millions of people called in to vote for Aiken. They kept him in the competition to the very end, and even then he only lost to Studdard by less than 1 percent of the vote.

13   During his weeks on the show, Aiken's image changed. He wore better clothes, got rid of the glasses, and began to look almost stylish. But more than anything, it was his smooth voice and his ability to sing with feeling that won him fans of all ages.

Fun Facts

▶ Aiken once let his students duct-tape him to the wall.

▶ His nickname is Gonzo.

▶ Aiken is his mother's maiden name, which he took after his parents separated.

Clay Aiken gives an inspiring performance during the final competition of *American Idol*.

14   Because the voting was so close, some of Aiken's fans wanted the votes counted again. But Aiken said "no" to that idea. He knew that Studdard had won fair and square. Besides, with or without the title of "American Idol," Aiken had proved himself to be a first-rate singer.

15   On October 14, 2003, he came out with his first album, *Measure of a Man*. It sold 613,000 copies in its first week, which sent it to the number-one spot on The Billboard 200. A few weeks later, the album topped two million in sales. This success made Aiken very wealthy.

16   One of the first things Aiken did was to buy two new cars. But he also used his money for something special. He created a foundation to help children with learning disabilities. He called it the Bubel Aiken Foundation. When Diane Bubel learned of the foundation's name, she was so honored she began to cry.

17   For Clay Aiken, starting a singing career has been wonderfully exciting, but it is the Bubel Aiken Foundation that is his dream come true. "I am in a position now to be a voice for people with developmental disabilities," he says. "I think all of us have a higher purpose for what we are doing."

A Understanding What You Read

◆ **Fill in the circle next to each correct answer.**

1. Aiken needed patience when working with Mike Bubel because

   ○ A. Mike's mother did not feel comfortable with Aiken.
   ○ B. Mike was too young to understand directions.
   ○ C. Mike has trouble communicating with people.

2. What caused Aiken to try out for *American Idol?*

   ○ A. He always knew he was a good singer.
   ○ B. A student's family encouraged him.
   ○ C. The foundation he worked for needed money.

3. Why did Aiken come in second place on *American Idol?*

   ○ A. More fans voted for someone else.
   ○ B. The judges voted for Ruben Studdard.
   ○ C. He didn't look like a pop star.

4. Which of the following statements is an opinion rather than a fact?

   ○ A. He began to look almost stylish.
   ○ B. He got a job helping autistic children.
   ○ C. He finished second to Ruben Studdard.

5. From what the article told you about Aiken, you can conclude that he is

   ○ A. happier being a well-known singer than being a teacher.
   ○ B. more focused on helping others than on being famous.
   ○ C. trying to get more people to audition for *American Idol*.

_____ Number of Correct Answers: Part A

B Finding the Main Idea and Supporting Details

◆ Read the paragraphs below. Fill in the circle next to the sentence that **best** states the main idea for each paragraph.

1.

One of the first things Aiken did was to buy two new cars. But he also used his money for something special. He created a foundation to help children with learning disabilities. He called it the Bubel Aiken Foundation. When Diane Bubel learned of the foundation's name, she was so honored she began to cry.

○ A. Aiken became wealthy very quickly.
○ B. Aiken used his money in specific ways.
○ C. Aiken made Diane Bubel very happy.

2.

He certainly didn't make a strong impression when he first walked onstage. He was tall and skinny, with funny glasses and a bad haircut. His shirt was not tucked in, and he was wearing big ugly shoes. People described him at this point as a "nerd" and a "geek." But his voice won over the judges. Said judge Simon Cowell, "You don't look like a pop star . . . but you've got a great voice."

○ A. Aiken managed to win over the judges with his voice.
○ B. Aiken didn't look much like a pop star when he tried out.
○ C. Some people did not understand why Aiken was on the stage.

_____ Number of Correct Answers: Part B

C Using Words

◆ **Complete each sentence with a word from the box. Write the missing word on the line.**

disabilities	flinch	regional
interacting	unconditional	

1. They made an _____ vow to honor each other.

2. The ramp at the door is for people with physical

_____.

3. He would rather be _____ with others than spending time alone.

4. The loud slam of the door made her _____.

5. The _____ airport served the southeastern part of the state.

◆ **Choose one word from the box. Write a new sentence using the word.**

6. word: _____

_____

_____ Number of Correct Answers: Part C

D Writing About It

Write a Postcard

◆ Suppose you had been in Atlanta, Georgia, trying out for *American Idol* with Clay Aiken. Write a postcard to a friend at home about your experience. Use the checklist on page 103 to check your work.

Dear _____,

   Today I stood in line with a guy named Clay. He told me he came for the tryouts only because _____.

He looked _____.

I didn't think he'd do well, but _____

_____.

       Sincerely,

_____

123 Main St.
Hometown, USA

Lesson 7 Add your correct answers from parts A, B, and C to get your total score. Then find the percentage for your total score on the chart below. Record your percentage on the graph on page 105.

_____ Total Score for Parts A, B, and C

_____ Percentage

Total Score	1	2	3	4	5	6	7	8	9	10	11	12	13
Percentage	8	15	23	31	38	46	54	62	69	77	85	92	100

Veronica Campbell

Running for the Gold

Birth Name Veronica Angella Campbell

Birth Date and Place May 15, 1982, Trelawny, Jamaica

Home St. Catherine, Jamaica

Think About What You Know

Have you ever felt so happy that you had to raise your hands in the air? What were you happy about? Read the article to find out what made Veronica Campbell very happy.

Word Power

What do the words below tell you about the article?

motivated inspired to take action

dutifully respectfully or obediently

semifinals the race that comes just before the final race

bonus something extra

emotional experiencing strong feelings

Reading Skill

Sequence The order of events in a story or an article is called **sequence.** The author will not always use signal words such as *first* and *then*. Sometimes you must use what you know and clues from the text to find the sequence.

Example

The First Event	When he was little, he seldom lost a running race against the kids in his neighborhood. In high school,
The Next Event	he was so fast that he was able to earn a college scholarship.

The first event in the sequence is "he seldom lost a running race against the kids in his neighborhood." The second event is "he was able to earn a college scholarship." How might you use the clues in the text and what you already know to find this sequence?

Veronica Campbell

Running For The Gold

Veronica Campbell wasn't hard to spot during recess at her school on the island nation of Jamaica. She was the one running the fastest. Campbell and some of the other children often played a game that involved dashing around trying to catch each other. "I used to do well at that," she says modestly. In Fact, Campbell could easily outrun any of her classmates, girls and boys.

2   One of the teachers noticed Campbell's speed and encouraged her to enter track-and-field competitions. "Mr. Collins was both my . . . teacher and coach," Campbell recalls. "He saw the potential, and he **motivated** me. He told me I would be able to do very well."

3   By the time she was 12 years old, Campbell was competing in real races. She even went to the Jamaican national championships for all ages. There she won two sprints, or short races, a performance that won her a scholarship to attend Vere Technical High School. Vere is famous for producing track stars such as Merlene Ottey, one of the greatest sprinters ever and a hero to Veronica Campbell. "She's my role model," Campbell says of Ottey. "I just like the way she runs and just everything about her."

4   Going to Vere was a terrific opportunity for Campbell, but it wasn't easy for her parents. "I remember in the early days when my mother would awake as early as 3:00 A.M. to get me on the bus to school," Campbell recalls.

5   When Campbell got to Vere, the coach instructed her to practice the 400-meter race. Campbell did as she was told, **dutifully** training for the 400. But she felt horrible running that race. "I never liked it," she says. "I would cry every evening." Luckily the coach finally switched Campbell over to the 100.

6   From there Campbell's track career took off. She was just 17 when she won the 100-meter sprint at the World Youth Championships. Then, in 2000, one of her dreams came true. She won a spot on Jamaica's 400-meter relay team. This meant she would compete in the Olympics held in Sydney, Australia. It also meant she would be on the same team as her idol, Merlene Ottey.

7   In the 400-meter relay, each team member runs 100 meters and then passes the baton to the next runner. With Campbell running the second leg and Ottey running the fourth leg, the team finished second. This made Ottey the oldest female athlete ever to win an Olympic medal. Campbell, 18 at the time, was one of the youngest.

8   Campbell now turned her attention to the 2004 Olympics to be held in Athens, Greece. There she hoped to win an individual medal. "Sydney was a great experience," she says, "and it really motivated me to try and get an individual medal."

9   Over the next four years, Campbell worked hard to get ready for Athens while still continuing her schooling. In 2001 she left Jamaica to attend college in the United States. First she went to a community college in Kansas, where she set many junior college track records, and then she moved on to the University of Arkansas, where she did more studying and training. During these college years, Campbell struggled with injuries. In one season she pulled a muscle, and in another she hurt her knee. Still, she never gave up her goal of running in the 2004 Olympics.

Skill Break

Sequence

Look at paragraph 5 on page 78. This paragraph tells about Campbell's training at Vere Technical High School.

Her coach told her to practice the 400-meter race. What happened next?

10   When the 2004 Olympic Games finally arrived, Campbell was ready. She was competing in three events—the 100-, the 200-, and the 400-meter relay. In the 100-meter **semifinals,** Campbell ran a great race, and it looked as though she was set to win a gold medal. But in the finals she stumbled just a bit and wound up finishing third. Still, the 200 was coming up, and that was the race she really wanted to win. As she put it, "The 100 is like a **bonus** race for me anyway. The 200 is what I've been focusing on all year."

11   In the 200-meter race, Campbell got off to a clean start. She took the lead on the curve and never gave it up. She dominated the field, winning in a personal best time of 22.05 seconds. "I knew I had the race won when I cleared the curve first," she says. When she crossed the finish line, she became the first Jamaican woman ever to win a gold medal in a sprint.

12   Back in Jamaica, thousands of people had crowded around TV and radio sets. When Campbell hit the finish line, they cheered wildly, hugged each other, and pumped their fists in the air. This was just the sixth time ever that Jamaica had won an Olympic gold medal.

13   When Campbell stood upon the victory stand, officials played the Jamaican national anthem. It was a special moment for Campbell, and tears welled up in her eyes. "I was very **emotional,**" says Campbell. "I was happy that I won, and I was so happy to hear my national anthem play."

Fun Facts

▶ Campbell has nine brothers and sisters.

▶ In the future, she hopes to be a teacher or to work in business.

▶ After the 2004 Olympics, Jamaican officials rewarded her with a new house.

Veronica Campbell raises her arms with joy as her team wins the Olympic gold medal in the 400-meter relay.

14   And Campbell wasn't done yet. There was still the 400-meter relay to run. Before that race she told her teammates that they needed to hear their national anthem again. The only way to do that, of course, was to win another gold.

15   This time Campbell ran the fourth leg. She and her teammates ran a nearly perfect race. Their time of 41.73 seconds set a new Jamaican record. Best of all, they captured the gold medal—and did so with a margin of victory that was the greatest in 20 years. Campbell is always humble about her accomplishments. She never boasts or makes a show of winning a race. This time, though, she allowed some of her joy to show. "For the first time in my life I held up my hands at the finish line," she says. "That is to show you how happy I was."

16   For the second time in less than a week, Campbell took the victory stand for the playing of the Jamaican national anthem.

17   "Jamaica should be proud of her," said one woman back in Jamaica. "This will put her right up there with Merlene Ottey."

Understanding What You Read

◆ **Fill in the circle next to each correct answer for questions 1, 4, and 5. Follow the directions shown for questions 2 and 3.**

1. Mr. Collins encouraged Campbell to compete in races because he

   ○ A. noticed her speed while she was playing games.
   ○ B. was the coach at Vere Technical High School.
   ○ C. wanted her to win another national championship.

2. Choose from the letters below to correctly complete the following statement. Write the letters on the lines.

   On the positive side, _____, but on the negative side, _____.

   A. Campbell struggled with injuries
   B. Campbell's mother had to wake up at 3:00 A.M.
   C. Campbell got a scholarship to Vere Technical High School

3. In which paragraphs did you find the information to answer question 2? Write the paragraph numbers on the line.

   _____

4. In 2000 one of Campbell's dreams came true when she

   ○ A. won her second gold medal in Athens.
   ○ B. continued her schooling in the United States.
   ○ C. ran the 400-meter relay with Merlene Ottey.

5. From what you read, which of these is probably true?

   ○ A. Campbell's favorite song is the Jamaican national anthem.
   ○ B. Campbell was honored to represent Jamaica at the Olympics.
   ○ C. Campbell's injuries have gotten in the way of her goals.

_____ Number of Correct Answers: Part A

B Finding the Sequence

◆ Read the paragraph below. It shows a sequence. Number the sentences below the paragraph to show the order of what happened.

1.

    Over the next four years, Campbell worked hard to get ready for Athens while still continuing her schooling. In 2001 she left Jamaica to attend college in the United States. First she went to a community college in Kansas, where she set many junior college track records, and then she moved on to the University of Arkansas, where she did more studying and training. During these college years, Campbell struggled with injuries. In one season she pulled a muscle, and in another she hurt her knee. Still, she never gave up her goal of running in the 2004 Olympics.

_____ Campbell set many junior college track records.

_____ Campbell went to a community college in Kansas.

_____ Campbell went to the University of Arkansas.

_____ Campbell left Jamaica to attend college in the United States.

◆ Reread paragraph 10 in the article. Campbell ran well in the 100-meter semifinals. Write what happened next.

2. _____

_____

_____ Number of Correct Answers: Part B

◆ The words and phrases in the list below relate to the words
in the box. Some words or phrases in the list have a meaning
that is the same as or similar to a word in the box. Some have
the opposite meaning. Write the related word from the box on
each line. Use each word from the box two times.

motivated	semifinals	emotional
dutifully	bonus	

Same or similar meaning

1. additional _____

2. openly feeling _____

3. without complaining _____

4. big race _____

5. faithfully _____

6. inspired _____

7. next to last _____

Opposite meaning

8. discouraged _____

9. lack _____

10. not expressing _____

_____ Number of Correct Answers: Part C

D Writing About It

Write a Journal Entry

◆ **Suppose you were at the 2004 Olympics and you watched Veronica Campbell run. Write a journal entry describing what you saw. Finish the sentences below to write your entry. Use the checklist on page 103 to check your work.**

Earlier this week, I saw Veronica Campbell win _____

_____.

Today Campbell and her team ran the 400-meter relay. Campbell

ran the _____,

and her team _____.

Campbell was so happy that at the finish line _____

_____.

It was really fun to watch.

Lesson 8 Add your correct answers from parts A, B, and C to get your total score. Then find the percentage for your total score on the chart below. Record your percentage on the graph on page 105.

_____ Total Score for Parts A, B, and C

_____ Percentage

Total Score	1	2	3	4	5	6	7	8	9	10	11	12	13	14	15	16	17
Percentage	6	12	18	24	29	35	41	47	53	59	65	71	76	82	88	94	100

Marc Anthony
Salsa Music Success

Birth Name Marco Antonio Muñiz

Birth Date and Place September 16, 1969, New York City

Home Brookville, New York

Think About What You Know

What kind of music did you listen to when you were younger? Do you still listen to the same music now? Read the article to find out how Marc Anthony learned to love the music of his childhood.

Word Power

What do the words below tell you about the article?

understandable clear or easy to see the meaning of

ballad a simple song about feelings or relationships

convention a formal meeting of members from a specific group

ovation an enthusiastic burst of cheering and clapping

reigning holding a position of power

Reading Skill

Author's Viewpoint An author's own feelings and beliefs are often shown in his or her writing. These feelings and beliefs are called the **author's viewpoint.** You can find clues about the author's viewpoint by paying attention to the author's choice of words.

Example

> Every part of the world has its own special music. Listening to music from an unfamiliar place can be an educational experience. You may discover new instruments, rhythms, and melodies. The world is full of so much wonderful and unique music. Explore!

In this paragraph, the author talks about listening to music from other parts of the world. The author's viewpoint is that *this is a positive thing to do.* One clue in the author's writing is the phrase "an educational experience." What are some other clue phrases?

Marc Anthony
Salsa Music Success

Marc Anthony grew up in the United States, but it took him a while to realize that was where he lived. "I thought I lived in Puerto Rico for the first seven years of my life," he says. The confusion was **understandable,** since Anthony's home life was filled with Puerto Rican culture. The food, the traditions, the music—all of it came from his parents' homeland of Puerto Rico. "My father had a rule," Anthony recalls. "For two days a week we had to speak Spanish in the house."

2   Anthony grew up with seven older brothers and sisters in the Spanish Harlem section of New York City. His father named him Marco Antonio Muñiz, in honor of a famous Mexican singer with the same name. Anthony would later change his name slightly to avoid being confused with this older performer.

3   Sing-alongs and Latin music called salsa filled the Muñiz household. But even in a family where everyone sang, it soon became clear that little Marco had special talent. When he was three years old, he learned a song about a native Puerto Rican bird. He would sing it while standing on the kitchen table. "He had just the one song," his father recalls, "but, boy, he could belt it out." The beauty of his voice caught everyone's attention. Once, after hearing him sing, his grown sister-in-law was so moved she began to cry. Anthony says that when he saw this, he thought to himself, "Hmm, there's something going on here."

4   Anthony's mother and father encouraged their son's musical dreams. But surprisingly, despite his Puerto Rican roots, Anthony's dreams didn't center on Latin music. "I rejected salsa at first," he admits. To him it was just something his parents played all the time at home. "Whenever I would hang out with my friends, I'd be like, 'Mom, would you turn that down?'"

5   Instead Anthony concentrated on singing in English. By the time he was a teenager, he was recording songs for advertisements, performing in nightclubs, and singing backup for other people's albums. None of this made him much money, though, and when he was 17 he decided to enter the Air Force. Two weeks before he was set to leave for boot camp, he was offered a record contract. Although the contract didn't offer a large amount of money, it was enough to make him abandon his plans for the Air Force.

6   Anthony's first big hit came in 1991, when he worked with Little Louie Vega on the album *When the Night Is Over*. The album itself didn't sell well, but one of the songs, "Ride on the Rhythm," quickly became a number-one dance hit in New York City.

7   A year later, the famous Latin American bandleader Tito Puente asked Anthony to serve as the opening act to his show in Madison Square Garden. Previously Anthony had only performed in dance clubs in front of a few hundred people, so this was a big step—and a successful one. The audience loved him, and Anthony loved the feeling of being a star. That ended his career of club singing. There was a much bigger world he now wanted to be a part of.

Skill Break
Author's Viewpoint
Look at paragraph 3 on page 88. The author talks about Anthony's voice. What is the **author's viewpoint** about Anthony's childhood voice? What phrases did you use as clues?

8   At this point, Anthony's manager suggested that he record something in Spanish, but Anthony wasn't interested. Then one day, he was listening to his car radio when a Spanish **ballad** came on. It was Juan Gabriel's version of "Hasta que te conoci," which means "Until I Met You." The song awakened something in Anthony's heart. "It ripped me apart," he recalls. "I don't know why, and I don't want to know why." All he knew was that he wanted to record a salsa version of this song.

9   When he did so, he discovered that salsa "was a bigger part of my life than I ever imagined." He says, "When it came time for me to sing it, I understood it without trying. I felt like I was in my house again."

10   After Anthony recorded "Hasta que te conoci," his manager made arrangements for him to perform it at a Latin music **convention.** The day didn't start out well. Most of the people in the audience were disc jockeys, and when Anthony walked onstage only one of them bothered to clap. Anthony tried not to let that disturb him. "Make believe you're singing in your living room to your mom," he told himself.

11   Anthony sang the song and then rushed off the stage, unaware that the audience was giving him a standing **ovation.** A few minutes later Anthony heard one of the disc jockeys talking on a cell phone. "Find this kid's CD," the disc jockey was telling someone back at his radio station. "I threw it out this morning. It's in the trash. Find it, and play it."

Fun Facts

▶ Anthony enjoys building model cars and planes.

▶ His nickname is Skinny.

▶ In 2004 he married singer and movie star Jennifer Lopez.

Marc Anthony took the traditional salsa music of his childhood and gave it his own style.

12   That same day, Anthony sang the song again on a Spanish-language TV show. People around the world fell in love with his music. Suddenly people couldn't get enough of this new singer. "That changed my life forever," says Anthony.

13   Anthony quickly became the hottest salsa singer around. People loved his voice, his passion, and his unique style. "When I decided to record salsa, I didn't want to mimic other salsa singers," he says. And he didn't. He developed a brand of salsa all his own. As one Latin music writer says, "He's a pop artist in salsa style."

14   Over the next 10 years Anthony released eight albums—six in Spanish and two in English. In 1998 he starred in a Broadway musical. He also began an acting career, appearing in such films as *Bringing Out the Dead* (1999) and *Man on Fire* (2004).

15   In 2004 Anthony won the Grammy Award for Best Latin Pop Album for *Amar sin mentiras (To Love Without Lies)*. Today Anthony has fans all around the world, and the *New York Times* has referred to him as "the **reigning** king of salsa." But one fan from Spanish Harlem says simply, "He is like a flame that walks."

A Understanding What You Read

◆ **Fill in the circle next to each correct answer.**

1. As a child, Anthony thought he lived in Puerto Rico because
   - ○ A. his family visited Puerto Rico all the time.
   - ○ B. he learned a song about a Puerto Rican bird.
   - ○ C. his home was filled with Puerto Rican culture.

2. What caused Anthony to begin recording salsa music?
   - ○ A. He was invited to sing at a Latin music convention.
   - ○ B. He was inspired by a Spanish song on the radio.
   - ○ C. His manager suggested that he sing in Spanish.

3. Which of the following categories would this story fit into?
   - ○ A. Stories from Puerto Rico
   - ○ B. Foolish Career Choices
   - ○ C. Singers with Natural Talent

4. Anthony became famous when he
   - ○ A. sang at a convention and on a TV show.
   - ○ B. left the Air Force and made an album.
   - ○ C. wrote songs in English and started acting.

5. What lesson about life does this story teach?
   - ○ A. It's best to speak more than one language.
   - ○ B. What you learn as a child can benefit you as an adult.
   - ○ C. Parents should let children choose their own music.

_____ Number of Correct Answers: Part A

B Finding the Author's Viewpoint

◆ Read the paragraphs below. Fill in the circle next to the sentence that **best** describes the author's viewpoint about Marc Anthony's music.

1.

    That same day, Anthony sang the song again on a Spanish-language TV show. People around the world saw him and fell in love with his music. Suddenly people couldn't get enough of this new singer. "That changed my life forever. I mean in one day," says Anthony. "I saw my old life shattered."

    Anthony quickly became the hottest salsa singer around. People loved his voice, his passion, and his unique style. "When I decided to record salsa, I didn't want to mimic other salsa singers," he says. And he didn't. He developed a brand of salsa all his own. As one Latin music writer says, "He's a pop artist in salsa style."

  ○ A. Anthony's music is wonderfully original.
  ○ B. Anthony's music changes all the time.
  ○ C. Anthony's music has too much passion.

◆ What clues helped you find the author's viewpoint? Write **three** clues on the lines.

2. _____

    _____

    _____

_____ Number of Correct Answers: Part B

C Using Words

◆ Cross out one of the four words in each row that does not relate to the word in dark type.

1. understandable

explain   know   see   give

2. ballad

song   cough   melody   listen

3. convention

confusing   meeting   gathering   discussion

4. ovation

applaud   cheer   write   perform

5. reigning

top   lost   queen   lead

◆ Choose one of the words shown above in dark type. Write a sentence using the word.

6. word: _____

_____

_____

D Writing About It

Write a Scene from a Play

◆ Write a scene from a play about Marc Anthony. The scene takes place right after Anthony's performance of "Hasta que te conoci" at the Latin music convention. Finish the sentences below to write your scene. Use the checklist on page 103 to check your work.

(Anthony walks backstage to where his manager is standing.)

Manager: Hey, nice job! That sounded great!

Anthony: Yeah? Man, I was so nervous. I had to _____

_____.

Manager: Whatever you did, it worked! There's a DJ in the

audience who's _____.

Anthony: Wow! I didn't think salsa _____

_____.

Lesson 9 Add your correct answers from parts A, B, and C to get your total score. Then find the percentage for your total score on the chart below. Record your percentage on the graph on page 105.

_____ Total Score for Parts A, B, and C

_____ Percentage

Total Score	1	2	3	4	5	6	7	8	9	10	11	12	13
Percentage	8	15	23	31	38	46	54	62	69	77	85	92	100

Compare and Contrast

◆ Think about the celebrities, or famous people, in Unit Three.
Pick two articles that tell about celebrities who showed talent as
children. Use information from the articles to fill in this chart.

Celebrity's Name		
How did the celebrity show talent as a child?		
Who encouraged the celebrity to develop the talent?		
How did the celebrity develop the talent?		

Glossary

A

achieve   to complete something successfully   p. 4

B

ballad   a simple song about feelings or relationships   p. 90

beloved   much loved   p. 7

bonus   something extra   p. 80

bungalow   a small house   p. 47

C

charity   a group that helps people in need   p. 16

chauffeur   a person who works as a driver   p. 36

comedy   the art of making people laugh   p. 5

contract   an agreed-upon plan   p. 16

convention   a formal meeting of members from a specific group   p. 90

culture   the beliefs and abilities of a group of people, passed along from one generation to the next   p. 25

cyclist   someone who rides a bicycle   p. 56

M

martial art   a type of fighting and self-defense, such as karate   p. 26

mentality   way of thinking or outlook   p. 57

miraculous   amazing or extraordinary   p. 56

motivated   inspired to take action   p. 78

N

naive   lacking knowledge about the way things work in the world   p. 37

nominated   suggested for an award   p. 7

O

ovation   an enthusiastic burst of cheering and clapping   p. 90

P

pelvis   the bones that support and protect the area of the lower stomach   p. 48

potential   a natural ability that might grow into something more   p. 17

R

regional   relating to a specific area or region   p. 69

reigning   holding a position of power   p. 91

rookie   a first-year player in a professional sport   p. 14

S

T

U

W

My Personal Dictionary

My Personal Dictionary

Writing Checklist

1. I followed the directions for writing.

2. My writing shows that I read and understood the article.

3. I capitalized the names of people.

4. I capitalized the proper names of places and things.

5. I read my writing aloud and listened for missing words.

6. I used a dictionary to check words that don't look right.

◆ **Use the chart below to check off the things on the list that you have done.**

✓	Lesson Numbers								
Checklist Numbers	1	2	3	4	5	6	7	8	9
1.									
2.									
3.									
4.									
5.									
6.									

Progress Check

You can take charge of your own progress. The Comprehension and Critical Thinking Progress Graph on the next page can help you. Use it to keep track of how you are doing as you work through the lessons in this book. Check the graph often with your teacher. What types of skills cause you trouble? Talk with your teacher about ways to work on these.

A sample Comprehension and Critical Thinking Progress Graph is shown below. The first three lessons have been filled in to show you how to use the graph.

Sample Comprehension and Critical Thinking Progress Graph

◆ **Directions:** Write your percentage score for each lesson in the box under the number of the lesson. Then put a small X on the line. The X goes above the number of the lesson and across from the score you earned. Chart your progress by drawing a line to connect the Xs.

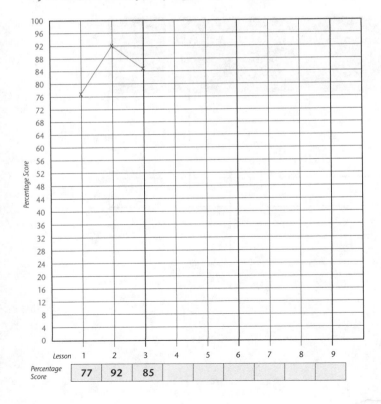

Lesson	1	2	3	4	5	6	7	8	9
Percentage Score	77	92	85						

Comprehension and Critical Thinking Progress Graph

◆ **Directions:** Write your percentage score for each lesson in the box under the number of the lesson. Then put a small X on the line. The X goes above the number of the lesson and across from the score you earned. Chart your progress by drawing a line to connect the Xs.

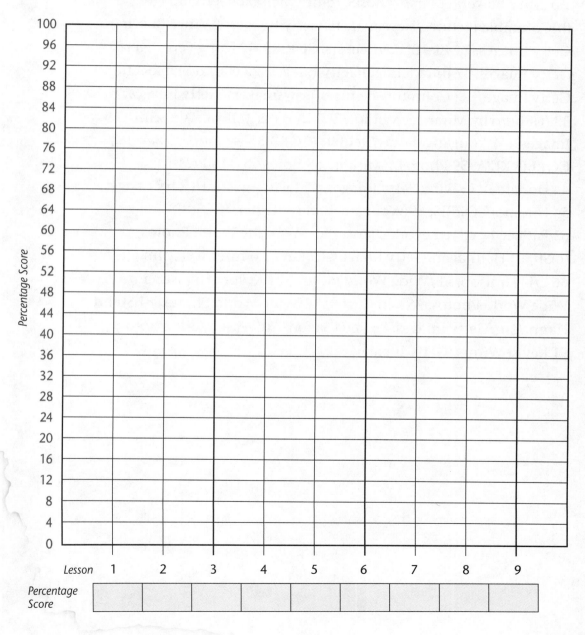

Photo Credits

Cover Dave Benett/Getty Images, (inset)Kevin Winter/Getty Images; 1 (t)Mike Blake/Reuters/CORBIS, (c)Jim McIsaac/Getty Images; (b)Columbia Pictures/Newsmakers/Getty Images; 2 Vince Bucci/ Getty Images; 7 Mike Blake/Reuters/CORBIS; 12 Doug Pensinger/ Getty Images; 17 Jim McIsaac/Getty Images; 22 Giulio Marcocchi/ Getty Images; 27 Columbia Pictures/Newsmakers/Getty Images; 33 (t)Photo by Miramax Studios/ZUMA Press, (c)Evan Agostini/Getty Images, (b)Wolfgang Rattay/Reuters/CORBIS; 34 Connan/Baverel/ CORBIS KIPA; 39 Photo by Miramax Studios/ZUMA Press; 44 Donald B. Kravitz/Getty Images; 49 Evan Agostini/Getty Images; 54 Duomo/CORBIS; 59 Wolfgang Rattay/Reuters/CORBIS; 63 Pat Lewis; 65 (t)Kevork Djansezian/AP/Wide World Photos, (c)Stuart Hannagan/Getty Images, (b)Kevin Winter/Getty Images; 66 Eric Jamison/AP/Wide World Photos; 71 Kevork Djansezian/AP/ Wide World Photos; 76 Ben Curtis/AP/Wide World Photos; 81 Stuart Hannagan/Getty Images; 86 Reed Saxon/AP/Wide World Photos; 91 Kevin Winter/Getty Images.